Soho Theatre and HighTide Festival Theatre present

PASTORAL

By Thomas Eccleshare

The first preview of *Pastoral* was at Soho Theatre on 25 April 2013.

Pastoral had its world premiere on 2 May 2013 at the HighTide Festival.

Soho Theatre and HighTide Festival Theatre are supported by Arts Council England.

Supported using public funding by
ARTS COUNCIL ENGLAND
LOTTERY FUNDED

AEM International
Arts Entertainment Media Executive Search

Supported by Clare Parsons & Tony Langham

CAST

MR PLUMB	Nigel Betts
MOLL	Anna Calder-Marshall
OCADO MAN	Bill Fellows
ARTHUR	Polly Frame
HARDY	Richard Riddell
BRIDE	Carrie Rock
MRS PLUMB	Morag Siller
MANZ	Hugh Skinner

CREATIVE & PRODUCTION TEAM

Thomas Eccleshare	Writer
Steve Marmion	Director
Michael Vale	Designer
Philip Gladwell	Lighting Designer
Tom Mills	Music and Sound
Nadine Rennie CDG	Casting Director
David Luff	Producer
Pam Nichol	Production Manager
Charlotte Bennett	Assistant Director
Dan Styles	Fight Choreographer
Steve Seymour	Associate Sound Designer
Sarah Mills	Costume Supervisor
Kate Schofield	Company Stage Manager
Ruthie Philip-Smith	Deputy Stage Manager
Nicola Morris	Assistant Stage Manager

Nigel Betts

Nigel has worked in theatre all over England including seasons at RSC, Bristol Old Vic, York, Cheltenham and the West Yorkshire Playhouse where he played Macduff. His other theatre credits include *Cyrano De Bergerac* at Lancaster; *The 39 Steps* in the West End; *War Horse* and *One Man, Two Guvnors* at the National Theatre. His TV credits include *Emmerdale*; *Coronation Street*; *EastEnders*; *Trial & Retribution*; *The Bill*; *The Catherine Tate Show*; *Holby City*; *Casualty*; *Midsomer Murders*; *A Touch Of Frost*; *Grease Monkeys*; *Inspector Lynley* and *Silent Witness*. Film credits include *Thunderpants, Paper Mask, The Whipping Boy, Desert Flower, Mrs Ratcliffe's Revolution* and *The Christmas Candle*.

Anna Calder-Marshall

Anna's theatre credits include *In the Republic of Happiness* at Royal Court; *Salt, Root and Roe* at Trafalgar Studios; *Danger: Memory: I Can't Remember Anything* at Jermyn Street; *The House of Bernarda Alba* at the Royal Exchange; *Love* at the Lyric Hammersmith; *A Kind of Alaska* at Gate Theatre; *Comfort of Apples* at Hampstead Theatre; *The Importance of Being Earnest* at Oxford Playhouse; *A Lie of the Mind* at Donmar Warehouse; *Antigone* at the Old Vic. Her TV and film credits include *Stage Door Johnnies* for Sky; *13 Steps Down, Midsomer Murders* and *The Bill* for ITV; *Holby Blue*; *New Tricks* and *Dalziel and Pascoe* for BBC; *Anna Karenina*; *Zulu Dawn* and *Wuthering Heights*.

Bill Fellows

Bill was born and bred in the industrial town of Middlesbrough where he was a apprentice fitter and turner before becoming a actor. His more recent TV credits include *Broadchurch*; *Downton Abbey*; *United*; *Land Girls*; *Hebburn*; *Waterloo Road*; *Casualty*; *George Gently* and is a regular in the award-winning children's drama *Wolfblood*. Bill's stage credits include playing Micky in the 1991 West End production of *Blood Brothers*; *Trackers* at the National Theatre; *Richard III* for Northern Broadsides; *Brassed Off* at Birmingham Rep and *Our Friends in the North* for Newcastle's Northern Stage. Film credits include *Silas Marner*; *The Tournament*; *In Our Name* and *Blackbeard*. Forthcoming films include the soon-to-be released *Harrigan* with Steven Tomkinson, the comedy drama *Tested* and the historical drama *King of Sands*.

Polly Frame

Polly trained at Bristol University. Her theatre credits include *After Miss Julie* at the Young Vic; *The Crossing – 66 Books* at the Bush Theatre; *The Comedy of Errors* at Stafford Shakespeare Festival; *Earthquakes in London* at the National Theatre; *The Count of Monte Cristo* at West Yorkshire Playhouse; *Macbeth* at Chichester, West End and Broadway; *Home-Work*, a Bodies in Flight production for Singapore Esplanade; *A Response to Twelfth Night*, a Filter production for the RSC; *The Prime of Miss Jean Brodie* and *Poor Mrs Pepys* at the New Vic; *ACDC* at Royal Court; *Cleansed* at the Arcola; *Who By Fire* and *Skinworks*, a Bodies in Flight production for Bristol Old Vic/touring; *Seven and a Half Minutes of Happiness*, *Di-sect* and *Eve* at the Bristol Old Vic.

Richard Riddell

Richard's recent theatre credits include *The Homecoming* directed by David Farr and *The Merchant of Venice* directed by Rupert Goold, both for the RSC. Further theatre includes *After the Party* at the Criterion; *Filumena* at the Almeida; *The Comedy Of Errors* and *Titus Andronicus* for Shakespeare's Globe. His television credits include: *Vera* (ITV); *A Warriors' Tale* (American World Pictures); *Misfits*, (Clerkenwell Films / E4); *The Fattest Man In Britain* (ITV); *Merlin* (Shine for BBC); *Krod Mandoon* (Hat Trick/Comedy Network); *Fanny Hill* (Sally Head Productions for BBC) and *Waking The Dead* (BBC). His film credits include: *Weekender* (Karl Golden); *Robin Hood* (Ridley Scott); *The Imaginarium of Doctor Parnassus* (Terry Gilliam); *Blitz* (Elliott Lester) and *Act of God* (Sean Faughnan).

Carrie Rock

Carrie's theatre credits include *Julius Caesar* at the Donmar Warehouse; *Treading Water* at Holloway Prison; *She From The Sea* at The Lift, Mobile Theatre; *Rondo, Hope and Anchor* at the Etcetera Theatre; *17 Minutes* at Soho Theatre; *Criminal Cabaret* at Brick Lane; *This Time Tomorrow* at Brighton Festival; *A WOMAN INSIDE* at Edinburgh Festival and *Sounds Like An Insult* written by Vivienne Franzman and performed at Amnesty International.

Morag Siller

Morag has recently appeared in *Orpheus Descending* and *After Black Roses* at the Royal Exchange and the BBC series *Moving On*. Other theatre credits include playing Rosie in *Mamma Mia*; *Top Girls* at Manchester Library; *Comedy of Errors* at West Yorkshire Playhouse; *Tons of Money* at the Bristol Old Vic; *Les Misérables* in the West End; *Blue Remembered Hills* at Sheffield Crucible and *Chatsky* at the Almeida. Films include *Memphis Belle*; *The Libertine* and *House of Mirth*. Other screen credits include *Monroe*; *Eternal Law*; *Marchlands*; *Lip Service* and a regular in *Jinx* for BBC. She has starred in both series of *Ladies of Letters* as Karen and has also starred in *Emmerdale* and regular characters in *Monarch of The Glen* and BBC's *Casualty*.

Hugh Skinner

Hugh's theatre credits include *Wild Oats* at Bristol Old Vic; *The Crossing – 66 Books*; *Where's My Seat*; *2 May 1998* and *Suddenlossofdignity.com* all at the Bush Theatre; *You Can't Take It With You* at the Royal Exchange; *'Tis Pity She's A Whore* at Liverpool Everyman; *Is Everyone OK?* with nabakov; *The Great Game* at the Tricycle Theatre; *Angry Young Man* at Trafalgar Studios; *The Enchantment* at the National Theatre; *Senora Carrar's Rifles* at Young Vic and *French Without Tears* at Yvonne Arnaud, Guildford. His film and TV credits include *Les Misérables* directed by Tom Hooper; *The Wipers Times*; *Law & Order*; *Any Human Heart*; *Tess of the d'Urbervilles*; *Bonkers* and *Day of the Dead*.

CREATIVE TEAM

Thomas Eccleshare WRITER
Thomas Eccleshare is a writer, performer and theatre maker trained at the Jacques Lecoq School. He is the co-artistic director of the award-winning visual theatre company Dancing Brick with whom he has toured work nationally and internationally, including the hit show *6.0: How Heap and Pebble Took on the World and Won*. Last year, Thomas won the Verity Bargate Award, a nationwide prize for emerging writers, for his first scripted play, *Pastoral*. He is currently writing TV sitcoms for Baby Cow Productions, Big Talk and Comedy Central. Thomas is the Pearson writer-in-residence at the Soho Theatre, for whom he is writing a second play.

Steve Marmion DIRECTOR
Steve is Artistic Director of Soho Theatre. For Soho Theatre, Steve has directed *Realism*, *Mongrel Island*, *Fit and Proper People*, *Utopia* and *The Boy Who Fell Into A Book*. Prior to joining the company in 2010, Steve directed *Macbeth* for Regent's Park Open Air Theatre and *Dick Whittington* for the Lyric Hammersmith. In 2009 he directed the highly successful production of Edward Gant's *Amazing Feats of Loneliness* for Headlong Theatre which received rave reviews on tour and at Soho Theatre. In 2008 he had three critically praised successes with *Vincent River* in New York, *Only the Brave* in Edinburgh and *Metropolis* in Bath. He also transferred Rupert Goold's *Macbeth* onto Broadway. Steve was assistant, then Associate Director, at the RSC over two years from 2006-07. In 2004 he directed several premieres for Sir Alan Ayckbourn at the Stephen Joseph Theatre and returned to direct the Christmas show in 2006. He has worked with the National Theatre, RSC, in the West End, on Broadway, at the Royal Court, Lyric Hammersmith, Theatre Royal Plymouth, Theatre Royal Bath, Watford Palace Theatre, Sherman Theatre Cardiff and Edinburgh Festival. *Only the Brave* (2008) was nominated for Best New Musical and Best New Music and his *Madam Butterfly's Child* (2004) and *Mad Margaret's Revenge* (2005) won the London One Act Theatre Festival.

Michael Vale DESIGNER

Michael has designed the sets and costumes for over 180 theatre and opera productions both in the UK and abroad including those he has directed. Companies he has worked with include: the RSC; the National Theatre; the Royal Opera House, Covent Garden; English National Opera; Glyndebourne Festival Opera; Opera North; English Touring Opera; De Vlaamse Opera, Antwerp; Los Angeles Opera; New Zealand International Art's Festival; Galaxy Theatre, Tokyo; Warsaw Globe Theatre Company; Munich Biennale; Lyric Hammersmith; Almeida Theatre; Soho Theatre; Manchester Royal Exchange; West Yorkshire Playhouse; Sheffield Crucible; Northampton Theatre Royal; Liverpool Playhouse; Nottingham Playhouse; Bristol Old Vic; Plymouth Theatre Royal; Edinburgh Royal Lyceum; Bolton Octagon; Oldham Coliseum; Manchester Library Theatre; Salisbury Playhouse; Colchester Mercury Theatre; English Touring Theatre; the Royal Festival Hall; the Queen Elizabeth Hall; The Sage, Gateshead; Battersea Arts Centre; Spymonkey; Kneehigh Theatre and Told By An Idiot, with whom he is an Associate Idiot. His work has been nominated for two Olivier Awards; an Irish Times Theatre Award; a Manchester Evening News Theatre Award; a Charrington Fringe First Award and an Off West End Theatre Award.

Philip Gladwell LIGHTING DESIGNER

Philip's theatre credits include *A Midsummer Night's Dream* at Bristol Old Vic; *Love The Sinner* at the National Theatre; *No Quarter, Oxford Street, Kebab* at Royal Court; *Before the Party* at the Almeida; *Miss Julie* at Schaubühne Berlin; *Limbo* for Underbelly/Australia/UK; *One For The Road, God of Carnage, Blood Wedding, Hedda Gabler* and *The Bacchae* at Royal & Derngate; *Cinderella, Aladdin, Mogadishu, Punk Rock* at the Lyric; *The Arthur Conan Doyle Appreciation Society, Melody, In The Bag* at Traverse; *The Spire, Design for Living* at Salisbury; *Small Hours* at Hampstead Theatre; *For Once* (Pentabus); *Further Than the Furthest Thing* (Dundee Rep, Winner Critics Award for Theatre in Scotland for Best Design); *Five Guys Named Moe* (Stratford); *Terminus* (Abbey Dublin/Australia/US/Young Vic/Edinburgh); *You Can't Take it With You, 1984, Macbeth* (Manchester); *The Wiz* (Birmingham /

WYP); *Thoroughly Modern Millie, Radio Times, Relatively Speaking, Daisy Pulls it Off, Blithe Spirit* (Watermill); *Gypsy, The King And I* (Leicester); *My Romantic History* (Bush/Sheffield); *Amazonia, Ghosts, The Member of the Wedding, Festa!* (Young Vic); and *Testing the Echo* (OOJ). Previous productions for Soho Theatre include *The Boy Who Fell Into a Book, Dandy in the Underworld, Shraddha, Overspill, Hot Boi!* and *Tape.*

Tom Mills MUSIC AND SOUND

Tom's theatre credits includes *Titus Andronicus* at RSC; *A Time To Reap, Wanderlust* at Royal Court; *Cesario, Prince of Denmark, The Eternal Not* at the National Theatre; *Comedy of Errors* at Cambridge Arts; *Cinderella, Aladdin, Dick Whittington* at Lyric Hammersmith; *The Alchemist* at Liverpool; *Boys, Clockwork, Dusk Rings A Bell* with HighTide; *Medea, A Midsummer Night's Dream, Edward Gant's Amazing Feats of Loneliness* with Headlong; *The Dark at the Top of the Stairs* at Belgrade Coventry; *The Littlest Quirky* on UK tour; *Benefactors, The Way of the World* at Sheffield; *Huis Clos, Lidless* at Donmar Warehouse/Trafalgar Studios; *Great Expectations, Moonlight and Magnolias* at Watermill; *Purple Heart, Wittenburg, Electra, Breathing Irregular, The Kreutzer Sonata, Unbroken* at the Gate; *Ahasverus* at Hampstead Theatre; *Pericles, Macbeth* at Regent's Park Open Air; *Elektra* at the Young Vic; *Ditch* at the Old Vic Tunnels; *The Grimm Brother's Circus, Metropolis, Oliver Twist* and *The Jungle Book* at Theatre Royal Bath. His other productions for Soho Theatre include *The Boy Who Fell Into a Book, Utopia, Mongrel Island* and *Realism.*

Charlotte Bennett ASSISTANT DIRECTOR

Charlotte is Artistic Director of Forward Theatre Project, associate company of Paines Plough. Directing includes *The Space Between Us; Swags and Tails* with Open Clasp at Live Theatre; *On the Harmful Effects of Tobacco/Can Cause Death* at the National Theatre; *A Five-Star Werewolf* at York Theatre Royal; *Blue/Orange* at Harrogate Theatre; *Comedy of Errors, Taming of the Shrew, Macbeth* with Sprite Productions and *Taketh Me Away* at Pleasance. Assistant directing includes English Touring Theatre and Bush Theatre.

 # HighTide Festival Theatre

MAKERS OF NEW THEATRE

"Terrific fount of new talent" *Metro*

HighTide Festival Theatre is one of the UK's leading producers of new plays, and the only professional theatre focused on the production of new playwrights. Currently we read and consider around 1000 scripts a year, from which we then work with 100 playwrights on a range of development opportunities, from workshops to full productions.

Under Artistic Director Steven Atkinson, we have premièred major productions by playwrights including Ella Hickson, Frances Ya-Chu Cowhig, Nick Payne, Adam Brace, Beth Steel, Laura Poliakoff, Luke Barnes, Vickie Donoghue, Lydia Adetunji and Joel Horwood.

We produce several productions a year in our annual Suffolk festival and on tour. Since 2007 we have staged over fifty productions, working with some of the world's leading theatres in London (including the National Theatre, Bush Theatre, Old Vic Theatre and Soho Theatre), regionally (including Sheffield Theatres, Watford Palace and Southampton Nuffield) and internationally (Public Theater New York and National Play Festival Australia).

HighTide have won two Fringe First Awards, four Corporate Engagement Awards, and many more nominations for leading literary awards.

Our 2013 Season includes the premiere of the Verity Bargate Award-winning *Pastoral* by Thomas Eccleshare (a co-production with Soho Theatre), *Smallholding*, the main stage debut play by Chris Dunkley (a co-production with Nuffield Theatre, Southampton), two European premieres: *Moth* by Declan Greene (transferring to the Bush Theatre) and *Neighbors* by the inaugural Tennessee Williams Award recipient Branden Jacobs-Jenkins (a co-production with Nuffield Theatre, Southampton), and Luke Barnes' acclaimed *Bottleneck* opens at Soho Theatre and then tours the UK. Later in the year we will premiere Jack Thorne's *Stuart: A Life Backwards* in the 2013 Edinburgh Festival (a co-production with Sheffield Theatres) and Phil Porter's *The Reprobates*, a new play for young people (a co-production with The Garage, Norwich).

"Famous for championing emerging playwrights and contemporary theatre" *Daily Mail*

London's most vibrant venue for new theatre, comedy and cabaret.

Bang in the creative heart of London, Soho Theatre is a major new writing theatre and a writers' development organisation of national significance. With a programme spanning theatre, comedy, cabaret and writers' events and home to a lively bar, Soho Theatre is one of the most vibrant venues on London's cultural scene.

Soho Theatre owns its own central London venue housing the intimate 150-seat Soho Theatre, our 90-seat Soho Upstairs and our new 1950s New York meets Berliner cabaret space, Soho Downstairs. Under the joint leadership of Soho's Artistic Director Steve Marmion and Executive Director Mark Godfrey, Soho Theatre now welcomes over 150,000 people a year.

'Soho Theatre was buzzing, and there were queues all over the building as audiences waited to go into one or other of the venue's spaces. I spend far too much time in half-empty theatres to be cross at the sight of an audience, particularly one that is so young, exuberant and clearly anticipating a good time.'
Lyn Gardner, *Guardian*

SOHO THEATRE BAR
Soho Theatre Bar is a vibrant, fun bar where artists and performers can regularly be seen pint in hand enjoying the company of friends and fans. Open from 9.30am until 1am, with free WiFi and a new, super quick and tasty burger, bagel, pizza and salad menu, Soho Theatre Bar is the perfect place to meet, eat and drink before and after our shows.

SOHO THEATRE ONLINE
Giving you the latest information and previews of upcoming shows, Soho Theatre can be found on facebook, twitter and youtube as well as at sohotheatre.com.

HIRING THE THEATRE
An ideal venue for a variety of events, we have a range of spaces available for hire in the heart of the West End. Meetings, conferences, parties, rehearsed readings and showcases with support from our professional theatre team to assist in your events' success. For more information, please see our website sohotheatre.com/hires or to hire space at Soho Theatre, email hires@sohotheatre.com and to book an event in Soho Theatre Bar, email sohotheatrebar@sohotheatre.com

Soho Theatre is supported by Arts Council England and Westminster City Council

Registered Charity No: 267234

Soho Theatre, 21 Dean Street, London W1D 3NE
sohotheatre.com
Admin 020 7287 5060
Box Office 020 7478 0100

PASTORAL

Thomas Eccleshare

PASTORAL

OBERON BOOKS
LONDON

WWW.OBERONBOOKS.COM

First published in 2013 by Oberon Books Ltd
521 Caledonian Road, London N7 9RH
Tel: +44 (0) 20 7607 3637 / Fax: +44 (0) 20 7607 3629
e-mail: info@oberonbooks.com
www.oberonbooks.com

A catalogue record for this book is available from the British
Library.

PB ISBN: 978-1-84943-444-7
E ISBN: 978-1-84943-828-5

Cover design: Michael Windsor-Ungureanu

Printed and bound by Marston Book Services Limited.

Visit www.oberonbooks.com to read more about all our books
and to buy them. You will also find features, author interviews and
news of any author events, and you can sign up for e-newsletters
so that you're always first to hear about our new releases.

Characters

MOLL
a very old woman

HARDY
a man, twenties

MANZ
a man, twenties

ARTHUR
an eleven-year-old boy

MR. PLUM
his father

MRS. PLUM
his mother

OCADO MAN

THE BRIDE

1.

A small flat with all the furniture removed. A door to the bathroom, a door to the bedroom and a front door to the hall. Upstage is a kitchenette with a window. On the window ledge are some flowers in a vase.

Grass, leaves and weeds are growing through the floorboards and under the doors.

In the only chair in the flat sits MOLL. By the door are two packed cases.

MOLL takes her handbag and slowly opens it.

Out of the handbag flies a fly. MOLL swipes at it and it disappears. She looks around her.

From her handbag she removes a compact mirror. She checks herself in the mirror. She replaces the mirror and withdraws from the bag a stick of lipstick, which she applies. Once finished she replaces the lipstick and checks the compact mirror again. She replaces the compact mirror and removes a tube of mascara from the bag, which she applies, carefully to each eye and then, having finished, checks the mirror. She replaces the compact mirror.

She removes from the bag an opened packet of pre-packaged fruit (anything that has been pre-sliced or pre-peeled will do). She eats the last of the fruit and places the empty pack in her bag.

She goes to the kitchenette. She picks up a food processor and places it in a large cardboard box. She opens a drawer, takes out an electric whisk and puts it in the cardboard box too. She unplugs the toaster on the kitchen top and puts it into the box. The kitchen is now bare.

She looks out of the window.

She looks back.

MOLL: Everyone out there is fat.

She looks out again.

Except…no, that's a lamp-post. Everyone out there is fat. There's four fat women, two fat men, five fat children and a fat infant. Suckling on her fat mum's breast. It's one of those milky, floppy breasts.

She mimes the breast.

She chuckles.

They're trying to jog. Bless them.

She takes a long sip of her tea.

She looks out again.

There's also a dog. A fat dog.

Pause.

Don't get me wrong, I've got nothing against the fat. Apart from on buses and planes. Or in lifts. Or in sexual situations, apart from with one another. I wouldn't want to get into a sexual situation with a fat. Not even on top. Imagine being in a sexual situation with a fat. Imagine it. It would be like being humped by a bouncy castle. A fat man: The breasts that flop. The wobbly flesh. The search for his prick in amongst the folds of wibbly flab. *(She mimes a bit.)* Having to flatten it out like a space on the beach so you can lie down.

A sip of tea.

No thanks.

She looks out again, this time for a bit longer.

Midsummer Place. A *place*. A *piazza*. Boots, Nandos, Gourmet Burger Kitchen. Zizzi. *(Enjoying the word, flirting.)* Zzzzizzi. I've not been.

Ever had a fat? Well exactly. I don't know how they reproduce.

A glance out.

Costa coffee's still open. A fat family sitting outside. *Al Fresco.* Like hippos in a swamp. They're being moved on.

I've got an order coming. Ocados. Bringing me my shopping. The good thing about Ocados is they'll shove it in colour coded bags. Cupboard, fridge…there's another one too. Cupboard, fridge. Red, purple…green. What's green? Anyway, Ocados're coming any minute with my weeklies.

(Looks out. Looks back at public, disgusted.) I mean fucking hell.

She drinks her tea.

Winston?… Pss, pss. Winston…?

Freezer! That's it.

She goes to the kitchen and gets a pre-packed cat food portion from a cupboard. She pulls off the silver foil sleeve and puts it on the floor.

She waits.

Last one. No more for Winston, no more for me.

Winston?

She looks out of the window again.

The family's gone.

There's another one though, outside the Haagen Dazs café. Skinny boy and two round parents. It's like they've been inflated.

Everything's growing.

Winston?

Silly mog.

There's a key in the door.

MANZ enters.

MANZ: Are you ready? Jesus, it's up here already.

MOLL: Was there anyone downstairs?

MANZ: No, they've gone.

MOLL: I told you. Everyone's going.

MANZ: Don't talk like that. They'll come back.

MOLL: How do you know?

MANZ: They left a note.

MOLL: Really? What did it say?

MANZ: They've gone on holiday. Just for a bit.

MOLL: Where to?

MANZ: Guernsey. Are you packed?

MOLL: I saw them leave.

MANZ: Moll.

MOLL: They had a lot of stuff.

MANZ: It's an adventure holiday. You need equipment.

MOLL: A couple of car loads at least.

MANZ: They're going potholing. You need all sorts for that. Come on.

MOLL: What's potholing?

MANZ: Hardy will be here soon and he'll want to be off.

MOLL: Is it like pottery?

MANZ: Have you packed?

MOLL: Or like pot?

MANZ: Moll?

MOLL: Or like moling?

MANZ: Moll. Are you ready?

MOLL: Nearly.

MANZ: Good girl. Don't look out there, it'll get your heart going. *(He sees the flowers.)* Christ!

He goes to the vase and tips the flowers out of the window. He washes the vase thoroughly then, thinking better of it, throws the vase out of the window too.

I'll help you finish packing up.

MOLL: Alright.

MANZ: What's left?

MOLL: A lot of the kitchen.

MANZ: Right.

MOLL: And the bathroom.

MANZ: Oh.

MOLL: And most of my bedroom.

MANZ: So what is done?

MOLL: I took care of Winston's basket.

MANZ: You sit down, I'll get started.

MOLL: Why did you say to pack the kitchen stuff? Doesn't Claire have kitchen stuff?

MANZ: She wants you to be comfortable.

MOLL: I don't mind borrowing hers. It would save me packing and repacking.

MANZ: She just wants you to be at ease.

MOLL: Well that's the idea of a holiday.

MANZ: Exactly.

MOLL: Does Claire not have furniture at her place?

MANZ: The furniture's different. It's going into storage.

MOLL: Storage? Just for while I'm away?

MANZ: That's what people do now. They rent their furniture when they go away, to fund the trip.

MOLL: Who hires furniture?

MANZ: Restaurants, hospitals, that sort of thing.

MOLL: And you said it was delivered alright?

MANZ: Come away from the window, it's scary for you out there.

MOLL: We could have left the furniture here.

MANZ: It's no trouble.

MOLL: They said you could collect it any time you liked?

MANZ: And we'll bring it back here just like it was.

MOLL: I tried cutting a few of the weeds.

MANZ: Hardy told you not to bother yourself with them. Let the army deal with all of this. They'll clean it up. I told you what they did in Southampton. I showed you the pictures didn't I? It was as good as new.

MOLL: A man came round on Tuesday.

MANZ: Which man?

MOLL: He said he was looking for you or Hardy.

MANZ: Oh. It must have been a friend.

MOLL: He wanted me to confirm that you and Hardy looked after me. I told him. I said we were related.

MANZ: That will be Jack. He's always playing practical jokes on us. Once he pretended that Hardy had been kidnapped. Tried to get me to pay a ransom. He's hilarious.

MOLL: Simms, it said on his card. He was an estate agent.

MANZ: Jack Simms. Yes, Hardy knows him. He probably thought Hardy would be here.

MOLL: He said Hardy had told him to come and have a look round and tell him what he thought.

MANZ: He's proud of you.

MOLL: Give him an evaluation.

MANZ: Look Moll. Things are dangerous here for you now. Everyone else in the building's leaving if they haven't already left. I'll take you to Mum's. It's safe there. She's concreted the field outside and built plastic walls around the concrete. It's all the latest stuff. You'll be happy there. And then, in a few weeks, once the army sort this mess out, we can come back here. It doesn't hurt to know what you're worth.

MOLL: There are butterflies in the sink. I think they're nesting. I told Simms and he didn't seem too pleased about it. Do you know Simms?

MANZ: He's Hardy's friend.

MOLL: He looks like a condom.

MANZ: I'm nearly done here. Why don't you relax on your chair while I finish the rest?

MOLL: I didn't go to my drawing class on Thursday.

MANZ: What? Why not?

MOLL: That branch had grown through the hall overnight. I couldn't climb over it.

MANZ: You mean you stayed here?

MOLL: Yes.

MANZ: You were here all morning?

MOLL: Yes. Simms dropped round again. He had a key. He said Hardy had given it to him as he wanted to show some people the flat. A young black couple. He was surprised to see me. I said they were welcome to look around and were they looking for something similar? They said yes. Simms talked about the army too, about how they'd clean up all the branches and leaves. Clear the square again. Which was a relief.

MANZ: It's just a precaution Moll. In case these weeds don't get sorted out. In case you can't come back. It's just in case. Have a rest.

MANZ goes to clear the bathroom. He clatters around.

MOLL goes to make tea. It's the final teabag. She looks out of the window again.

MOLL: They first noticed it a few weeks ago, creeping round the war memorial and through the crack outside Subway. Just little weeds at first, little sprouts. Herbs and reeds and wild mushrooms. It's amazing how quickly they're growing though, I have to admit that.

She puts the tea on.

Where's Ocados? I'd murder a Pepperami.

She looks out of the window.

They must be freezing. Though I suppose the blubber protects them a bit. Why haven't they moved on? Someone should tell them it's dangerous. Everyone's moving. Maybe they can't lift themselves up.

Pause.

I'm working on a joke.

I've got the punchline, it's just a matter of working out the first bit. Well, not so much the punchline, but I know what I want to be the butt. The butt of the joke, I've got that all worked out. Hen nights. I've been thinking of one of those, 'such and such walked into a bar' formats.

A group of whales walk into a bar. *(Beat.)* It's a hen night.

Or, hang on. Seven drunk gorillas walk into a bar. *(Beat.)* It's a hen night. Hm. A number of drunk… A number of…

Needs work.

Knock knock. Who's there? Slags. Slags who? *(Pause.)* Just some slags on a hen night. Are at the front door.

It's coming.

Here's a hen night now, being shepherded through the square. Looks like it's over before it's begun. We get a lot of hen nights. And even more over the last week. Everyone's getting married. Flash weddings, like during a war. There's fifteen of them! Fifteen! Dressed in pink. Original. And they've got fairy wings. Optimistic to think those wings will get those bodies off the ground. You'd need a forklift truck.

Who've we got? They have names on the backs of their shirts, you see. 'Superslag', 'Attila the Slut', 'Queen Dicktoria', 'Pink Fairy', 'Lady Bra Bra'. 'Liz'. Not very imaginative, Liz. 'The Boobmonster', 'Boobatron', 'Baron Von Boob', 'Napoleon Bonatart'. You get the idea. And here's the bride! To be fair, she is a good looking girl. Blonde and firm in all the right places. And on her T-shirt, hold on, she's got a special message. 'Buy me a shot, 'cos I'm tying the knot'. That's so sweet. Oh, and on the back... 'I'm the hen. Ask me to lay an egg'. I'm not sure I even know what that means. Vodka Revolution's closed. No party for you.

MANZ re-enters with a filled-up case.

MANZ: Moll, please.

MOLL goes to the chair.

MANZ goes to the bedroom.

MOLL looks at herself again in her compact mirror. An ant crawls onto her hand. She watches it crawl over her finger for a bit, then brushes it onto the floor and stamps on it, hard.

She falls asleep.

There is a key in the door. HARDY enters.

He sees MOLL asleep.

MANZ re-enters.

MANZ: Well?

HARDY: I've got the van downstairs. I had to park in St Luke's; the car park here's been torn to shreds. There's a willow come straight through it, squirrels and birds everywhere.

MANZ: I saw a deer on my way here.

HARDY: We need to go.

MANZ: Do you think we should wake her?

HARDY: Give it ten minutes, then I will.

MANZ: Where are you going to go?

HARDY: Sophie's parents have a shower on the ground floor.

MANZ: And space?

HARDY: How much will she take?

MANZ: Do they have a garden?

HARDY: They've concreted it over. Then tarmacked the concrete. It will be night, soon. No sun. We should get there before sunrise; they'll be stronger in the sun.

MANZ: Which route are you taking?

HARDY: I'll go out over Radburton, head north up the A11.

MANZ: They just closed the A11.

HARDY: Not five minutes ago they hadn't.

They get out their phones and check.

HARDY: Shit.

MANZ: She thinks she's going to stay with my mum. For a holiday.

HARDY: Good. *(To himself.)* I'll take the B road then. Shit.

MANZ: She'll be disappointed.

HARDY: She'll get over it. It's for her own good. I told you she should have left days ago. The whole of the South's gone. Have you seen London?

MANZ: I showed her an old picture of Southampton. Told her it was after the army had cleared up.

HARDY: Hope's good for her.

MANZ: She met Simms.

HARDY: It doesn't matter now. He can't do anything, it's too late.

MANZ: I saw a vole earlier.

HARDY: Where?

MANZ: Coming out of Paperchase. It was strutting.

HARDY: I believe it. There was a rabbit warren at the bottom of Aldi almost a week ago. I saw a rabbit by the yoghurts. I walked right up to it and it just sat there. We looked at each other but it didn't move. I got to less than a metre away before it darted. How did they get a warren into Aldi? No one did anything about it. No one ever does anything about anything.

MANZ: What could they have done?

HARDY: Re-tiled? Extermination? Poison? What do people normally do? What have we been doing?

MANZ: Who knows? We thought we had time. They've been too quick for us and now it's escalated.

HARDY: Even two days ago I was still eating fruit. I cut into an apple and it fell apart with worms and maggots. I was sick. Fell apart in my hand with worms and maggots.

MANZ: We should wake her.

HARDY: Everything teeming with life.

MANZ: I could take her, if you like.

HARDY: You? Where would you take her?

MANZ: I could take her to Mum's. It's further but she knows her at least.

HARDY: I'll take her. Is it night yet?

MANZ goes to the window.

MANZ: The moon's up. It's shining on the grass in the square; wood rush and reedmace sprouting through the cracks. Trees now too.

HARDY: Sycamore?

MANZ: Not yet. Ash and oak saplings over bluebells and wood sorrel. The pavement outside Nandos has cracked open and there's a brook. Herons, kingfishers and ragged pondweed.

HARDY: We need to go. *(Gently.)* Moll? Moll.

MOLL: *(Waking.)* I'm here.

HARDY: It's time to go. I've got the van downstairs. I'll carry you down alright.

MOLL: Where's Winston? I don't want to go without Winston.

HARDY: He'll be fine Moll, he'll be here when you get back.

MOLL: Still, I'd like to take him. Can't we take him?

MANZ: You go down to the van with Hardy Moll. I'll find Winston and bring him down with me.

MOLL: Alright. Isn't there time for me to have a quick bath?

HARDY: They're closing Grafton Road in half an hour. We have to go *now*.

MOLL: I'll just get my handbag. Ah! Ah! A spider! As big as my hand.

MANZ: I'll get it.

HARDY: Use a glass.

MOLL: Jesus. It has flesh on its legs!

MANZ: Where's it gone?

They look for it.

HARDY: It must have crawled back where it came from.

33

MANZ: Spiders.

HARDY: Mice'll be next. Then badgers. Let's go.

MOLL: Well, goodbye flat. See you shortly. Good luck.

There is a knock on the door.

MOLL: Ocados! I told you they'd come.

MOLL goes to the door and opens it.

Into the room walks a chubby young boy, ARTHUR, holding a toy knight's sword.

He stands in the middle of the room, looking around.

Silence.

MOLL: He looks too young to drive a van. What's your name?

ARTHUR: Arthur.

MOLL: Like the king?

ARTHUR: No.

MOLL: Is that your sword?

ARTHUR: Yes.

MOLL: What do you have a sword for?

ARTHUR: It's just a toy. It's not real.

MOLL: Where are your parents?

ARTHUR: Knocking on doors too.

MOLL: Are you selling something? Would you like me to buy something?

ARTHUR: No.

HARDY: Why are you knocking on doors? It's dangerous out there.

ARTHUR: My mum told me to.

HARDY: And who told her to? Was it the policemen?

ARTHUR: Yes.

HARDY: Where?

ARTHUR: Haagen Dazs.

MANZ: Why didn't you go home?

ARTHUR: Because we're going on an adventure away from home. It's my job to be brave and find a place to camp.

MOLL: Like a knight in shining armour.

ARTHUR: Yes.

MOLL: Well you can stay here.

MANZ: Moll. We have to try to leave ourselves.

HARDY: Why didn't you go to the other floors? The other towers?

ARTHUR: This is my special building. I'm supposed to try this building cos it's the biggest and I'm the bravest of us three.

HARDY: Didn't you try the floors below?

ARTHUR: They're all locked. I tried to break in but I couldn't. Do you have any crisps?

MANZ is at the window.

MANZ: The army's in the square. The roots have come right through now, grass as high as the bollards. They've cordoned off the entrances.

HARDY: Shit.

MANZ: It's too late. They've roped off Arlington Way. They must have quarantine the whole block.

MOLL: Go and get your parents. Tell them you've found a special place to camp.

2.

i)

The same flat. The next evening.

A huge oak has burst through the floorboards. The leaves and grass under the doors and floor are longer and denser.

MOLL, HARDY, MANZ, ARTHUR and MR. and MRS. PLUM are there. MR. and MRS. PLUM are both plump. There is a plate with some biscuit crumbs on it.

Silence.

MOLL: At least it'll look nice in Autumn.

MRS. PLUM picks up the plate and licks it clean.

When she has thoroughly licked it she passes it to her husband. He takes it and gives it another licking. He places it on the floor.

MRS. PLUM takes it up again and begins to lick.

ARTHUR: Can we order a pizza?

MR. PLUM: I told you Moll's already got food on the way Arthur. It'll be here soon.

Pause.

HARDY: Manz and I should go down there.

MOLL: It must be the roads that are keeping them. I can see from here, the roads are at a standstill. I've got a big order, it'll be enough for all of us.

MANZ: Moll, no one's coming in or out. Not even Ocados.

MRS. PLUM: Are they usually prompt?

MOLL: They're usually very prompt. I can see though, it's chaos down there. I can see why they would be delayed.

MRS. PLUM: Perhaps you could call them. See if there's anything you can do?

HARDY: Everyone looked the other way. We should have been evacuating days ago.

MOLL: Things shot up. We've been ambushed.

MANZ: *(At the window now.)* The square's gone. I can actually see it growing.

MOLL: They only pedestrianised it a few years ago, when Eat was still Our Price. They needn't have bothered!

MANZ: It's a copse now. Ash and oak and hazel all densely packed in.

HARDY: What do you say Manz, let's go down?

MOLL: First it was just one, a few weeks ago, a sapling by the war memorial.

MANZ: I can't see the cobbles, just leaves and branches.

MOLL: The noise of the birds will keep me up. Not to mention the fucking squirrels.

ARTHUR laughs.

MANZ: The glass in the front of Paperchase has been smashed through. A birch has come straight up through it in the space of an hour.

MR. PLUM: Perhaps we should try the stairs again?

ARTHUR: Where's uncle Tim? Is he at home still?

MRS. PLUM: Yes Arthur. He's safely at home.

ARTHUR: Why was Daddy trying to call him all the time?

MRS. PLUM: Daddy wanted to tell him what a fun time we're having here.

ARTHUR: Wouldn't he want to come on the adventure?

MRS. PLUM: Uncle Tim has a bad back. He wouldn't like this sort of adventure.

ARTHUR: Why were you crying before?

MRS. PLUM: That's enough Arthur. Here, why don't you play on your PSP for a bit?

ARTHUR: I've clocked it. It's boring now. Does she have internet?

MRS. PLUM: I don't know love, why don't you ask her yourself. Politely.

ARTHUR: Excuse me. Have you got internet?

MRS. PLUM: Internet what?

ARTHUR: Sorry. Wireless internet.

MRS. PLUM: Wireless internet *please.*

ARTHUR: Wireless internet please.

MOLL: The roots have torn up the cabling. You'll have to do it the old-fashioned way.

ARTHUR: What does that mean?

MOLL: Magazines.

MOLL and ARTHUR smile.

MRS. PLUM: They were still doing the square when we got married, I remember because we'd planned to go through there on the way back from the service but there was all sorts of rubble and tractors and things. Do you remember Clive?

MR. PLUM: That's right.

MRS. PLUM: It was a very nice wedding indeed, I have to say. Very tastefully done. David Scott from interflora did the decorations for us. Sweet peas, 'Show Girl' peonies, spray roses and lavender. Then senecio, rosemary and peppercorns too on the tables. It was lovely.

MANZ: There's lights coming from the square. People are gathering. Looters, I think.

HARDY: Let's go.

MOLL: Don't. Wait here. Ocados will come. You'll see.

MANZ: We won't risk more than half an hour. We'll be careful.

HARDY: If we don't go now everything will be snatched.

MOLL: I'm sure Ocados will come.

HARDY: Moll, it's alright.

He takes a gun from his bag.

MOLL: Where did you get that?

ARTHUR: Wow.

HARDY: I thought I might need it.

MOLL: Why?

HARDY: To shoot something. Look, if we don't get food soon, we'll starve, or be too weak to stand a chance.

MOLL: But –

HARDY: Moll.

ARTHUR: Can I come?

They look at him.

ARTHUR: I want to use the gun.

HARDY: No.

ARTHUR: I can be brave. Tell him, Dad.

MANZ: You stay here. We need some of our best people here, to protect Moll.

MR. PLUM: I should go with the boys.

MRS. PLUM: No, Clive, you stay. There's no point in everyone going.

MANZ: I can hear people shouting.

MR. PLUM: Perhaps you're right. We'll hold the fort here.

MRS. PLUM: Exactly. Stay here with Arthur, that's your job. We'll stay here for Arthur.

HARDY: Come on.

They leave.

ii)

ARTHUR and MOLL are in the room alone.

MOLL is dozing. ARTHUR is climbing in the branches of the tree.

MOLL wakes.

MOLL takes out a cigarette and lights it. She smokes.

The sound of rustling stops. Suddenly, he swings, upside down, hanging by his knees, looking at the old woman.

He stares at the cigarette.

MOLL: Where are your parents?

ARTHUR: Having a bath.

MOLL: They went home? How?

ARTHUR: No.

MOLL: They're having a bath here?

ARTHUR shrugs, upside down. MOLL shivers.

ARTHUR: Can I nick a fag?

MOLL: You're a bit young to smoke.

ARTHUR: I'm not that young. I just look young to you because you're so old.

MOLL: How old are you?

ARTHUR: Eleven. *(She moves the cigarette away.)* And a half.

Pause.

She holds the cigarette forward. He swings down and eagerly takes it from her.

He begins to smoke.

She takes out another cigarette and lights up.

MOLL: Well?

ARTHUR: Thank you.

They sit together, smoking. At length they finish.

ARTHUR: Shall we twos another?

She takes out another and lights it.

She passes it to ARTHUR.

ARTHUR: Thank you.

They pass it between each other, taking a few drags at a time.

ARTHUR: You've not got anything harder? Any weed? Skunk? Any coke?

MOLL: I've got some smack in the fridge.

ARTHUR: Really?

MOLL: No. I have Yakult, it's the only thing left. Will that do?

ARTHUR goes to get the Yakult.

ARTHUR: Do you want one?

MOLL: Yes.

ARTHUR: Who are those boys?

MOLL: They look after me.

ARTHUR: Why?

MOLL: Obligation.

ARTHUR: What does that mean?

MOLL: Guilt.

ARTHUR: Are they your sons?

MOLL: No.

ARTHUR: Are they your toy boys?

MOLL: No.

ARTHUR: Do you love them?

MOLL: No.

ARTHUR: Do you love anyone?

MOLL: Yes.

ARTHUR: Who?

MOLL: Myself.

ARTHUR: Have you ever been in love with someone not including yourself?

MOLL: Of course.

ARTHUR: Who?

MOLL: Paul Newman.

ARTHUR: Who's that?

MOLL: Another knight.

ARTHUR: Are you married?

MOLL: Not any more.

ARTHUR: When were you married?

MOLL: Never. I just said not any more to make sure you didn't feel sorry for me.

ARTHUR: Have you been in love though yeah?

MOLL: Yes. Everyone's been in love.

ARTHUR: In the war?

Pause.

I remember the first time I fell in love. It was in Campbell Park, down by the canal. They'd boarded up the adventure playground because it wasn't safe. Me and Cal were hitting up the boards on the canal side, where no one's around. I got bored so me and Cal walked round the park a bit. Nicole Clark was standing, leaning against the railings of the running track. I knew her because she used to go to my school, but she left last year to go to secondary. She's one of the most beautiful girls in the world, with massive tits and a really pretty face. We went up to her and Cal asked her for a cigarette. She laughed at Cal's face and I started laughing too. Cal got all annoyed and stormed off, calling me names. I stayed standing next to Nicole though and we just stood there in silence. It was dead pretty. I looked at her and touched her leg. Like this. She's a bit taller than me, because she's older, but I just stood there touching her leg. It was really nice and really warm and I just stood there, falling in love. She didn't look at me, so I began to feel up her leg. I could feel her pants, soft like a cushion, and when I put my fingers inside her pants I could feel her hair, which was a bit of a surprise. That's when I knew I was in love. It was like a song or something, when you feel your heart go. I started to finger her a bit, just stick two fingers in and out, but my arm hurt from holding it upright so I stopped. It's the best feeling in the world, love.

MOLL: Yes. That sounds very nice. Love can be a beautiful thing.

ARTHUR: The adventure playground's not there anymore. It's just park. The train tracks too. Are you sure you're not in love with those boys? Do you think they can get some weed for me?

MOLL: Plants are dangerous.

ARTHUR: When they come back I'll ask them if they can get some weed for me.

MOLL: What's going on out there?

ARTHUR runs to the window but can't see out. He drags a chair over, climbs onto the chair, and from there onto the kitchen surface. He looks out of the window.

ARTHUR: It's night. There are lights though, from machines I think. Looks like some machines have come in. I can't see much. There are some soldiers or firemen or something talking in Tesco pointing at the trees. I think they're trying to chop them down. There's a soldier with a chainsaw trying to clear the door to Vision Express.

MOLL: Are the boys down there?

ARTHUR: Which boys?

MOLL: The boys that were here before? Are they down there?

ARTHUR: Didn't I just say, I could only see machines and soldiers and all the trees. Can I have another Yakult?

MOLL: Yes.

ARTHUR: I like your hair. It's like silver.

MOLL: Thank you. I like yours. It's like gold.

ARTHUR: Who's King Arthur?

MOLL: He was a king who lived a very long time ago. When England was all covered in woods and forests. He had a lot of knights who fought for him and a wife called Guinevere.

ARTHUR: Was she buff?

MOLL: Yes. He had a sword like that one that he pulled from a stone, which is how people knew he was king.

ARTHUR: I got this at Toys 'R' Us. I put it in my school bag and walked out.

MOLL: They didn't have Toys 'R' Us then. His sword was better than yours anyway.

ARTHUR: Did you know him?

MOLL: Not personally.

ARTHUR: What was Guinevere like?

MOLL: Gentle and kind.

ARTHUR: Blonde?

MOLL: I don't know.

ARTHUR: Probably blonde. What did they do, the knights?

MOLL: They fought and ate and rode horses round the forests.

ARTHUR: Cool.

MOLL: Do you have any knights?

ARTHUR: I had Cal. But he left in class six because his dad works in Coventry.

MOLL: Poor thing.

Silence.

ARTHUR: Are the boys your knights?

MOLL: Sometimes. I don't really have any either.

ARTHUR: What does Moll mean?

MOLL: Nothing. It just sounds nice.

ARTHUR: I like it.

MOLL: Yes. It's not a real name though, like Arthur. That's a real name.

Pause.

ARTHUR: I'm hungry.

MOLL: Me too.

ARTHUR: I wish I could have gone down with the boys, with the gun. I would have got you something to eat.

Silence.

There's a turn in the lock and the door opens. HARDY and MANZ enter.

MR. and MRS. PLUM come in wearing towels.

MR. PLUM: Here we go.

MRS. PLUM: At last!

MOLL: What took so long? Did you find anything?

The boys look defeated.

Did you loot anything for me?

HARDY: It's all gone. All been taken.

MRS. PLUM: What about Nandos? Did you try Nandos?

MANZ: Stripped. There's nothing left.

MR. PLUM: What are we going to do?

MRS. PLUM: Don't be greedy, Clive. I'm sure they did their best.

MOLL: Did you manage anything?

MANZ reveals a mangled Boots bag and hands it to MOLL.

She takes from it a lipsalve stick, some paracetemol, another lipsalve stick, and a third lipsalve stick.

MANZ: Sorry.

HARDY: It's chaos down there. When we came out into the square it was like being in a forest. Underneath our feet the stones, the old paving stones have been ripped up. There were lights from somewhere, and they'd already tried getting the machines close enough to do some damage, but nothing was working. We managed to find our way to Wagamama. Branches had smashed through the windows, and in the restaurant the floor had been ripped up by cotton grass and pond sedge. Someone had looted a gas cylinder from the kitchen and was trying to get it lit, trying to burn down the wood, but it wouldn't catch. We skirted round the square, keeping to the outside. The middle was so dark, just shadows of looters, and howls of people lost in there. Bonfires were springing up round the outside, people piling the paper and folders out of Rymans and burning them up, trying to make it catch the edge of the forest, but it's not working. Nothing's working. Eventually we found Tescos, but it had all gone. A couple of rotten ready meals left on the till, an empty can of Lilt in the fridge. Apart from that: nothing. Cleaned out. The floor was smeared with smashed pasta sauces and microwave shepherd's pies, dotted with footprints from jackboots and deer. We got to Boots, but it wasn't much better. We took what we could.

They look at the lipsalves. Pause.

ARTHUR: Did you go to Game?

HARDY: Eh?

ARTHUR: Did you go past Game at all?

HARDY: On Hills Road? That's ten minutes away.

ARTHUR: It's just, I thought you might have picked me something up. *(He holds up his PSP.)*

There's a scratching on the door.

MOLL: Ocados?

She goes to open the door.

HARDY: Careful.

She looks through the peeper.

MOLL: It's Winston!

HARDY: Don't open the door.

MOLL: What do you mean? It's Winston.

HARDY: You didn't see it down there. They're not scared of us any more. You don't know who he's with.

MOLL: I can see, look he's on his… *(She fades out to silence.)*

MANZ: What?

MOLL: There's another cat with him. A ginger Tom.

HARDY: Moll. Do not open that door.

MOLL: They're both there, looking at the door. Winston's looking at me. I want to let him in.

MRS. PLUM: Please don't open the door. I'm afraid. And Clive is allergic to cats.

MR. PLUM: It's not bad, but they do irritate my skin.

MOLL: Winston! There's more, four of them now. They're all there, lying outside the door. And another, coming down the stairs. A big tabby. They're looking at me.

MANZ: We can't let them in, Moll.

MOLL: He's my cat.

HARDY: Not any more.

MOLL: Winston.

3.

i)

A dense wood. The next day. All that remains of the flat is MOLL's chair.

MANZ, MOLL, ARTHUR and his parents are there, famished and weak. HARDY is elsewhere.

MRS. PLUM is holding WINSTON's tin of catfood. It's now empty. She runs her finger along the inside and sucks it. There's nothing left.

MANZ: Do you know how to build a fire?

ARTHUR: I'm hungry.

MANZ: This will take your mind off it. Have you made a fire before?

ARTHUR: Me and Cal once made flame throwers from his step-brother's Lynx.

MANZ: The important thing is to make sure you've got all the big bits at the bottom and then the smaller bits, the twigs, on the top, in a wigwam. There.

ARTHUR: I'm hungry.

MR. PLUM: I'm sure Hardy will be back soon.

ARTHUR: What will he bring?

MR. PLUM: Whatever he can catch.

ARTHUR: I hope he brings Subway.

MANZ: Where are the matches?

MR. PLUM: We had two packs… Here. Ah! Ants. The box is filled with ants.

MANZ: And the matches?

MR. PLUM: Gone.

MANZ: Where's the other box?

They scurry to look for the box.

ARTHUR: Here!

They huddle round the box. He's about to open it.

MR. PLUM: Let Manz do it darling.

ARTHUR hands it to MANZ.

Slowly, he pokes the matchbox open.

They breathe a sigh of relief.

ii)

The same, later. Still no fire.

ARTHUR: Are you hungry?

MOLL: Yes. Are you?

ARTHUR: Yes. But I'm trying to be brave.

He picks up a leaf from the ground. He tries to bite into it, but it's too tough.

MANZ is trying to get the fire going with a packet of matches.

MOLL: Don't waste them. You're wasting them. Wait till Hardy gets back, he'll do it.

MANZ: I can do it.

MOLL: You're not having much luck.

ARTHUR: Mum, I'm hungry.

MANZ: Fuck! Fucking stupid, shit matches. Fucking fire.

ARTHUR: Dad! When will he be here?

MRS. PLUM: Try again Clive.

MR. PLUM: Why? What's the point? There's no signal. The canopy's blocking it out. Or birds have got to the lines and pecked them out.

MRS. PLUM: What's the harm in trying?

MR. PLUM takes his phone and holds it up, looking for signal. He follows it round, like a gold prospector, holding it up and down. He searches around the copse.

MR. PLUM: Happy?

iii)

They all sit. They are almost drunk with hunger.

The fire has been scattered, unlit, as if kicked apart.

MANZ is fuming, pacing around.

MRS. PLUM: I tell you what's amazing. That someone actually *invented* ovens. Do you see what I mean? Once there weren't ovens. Then there were. Someone must have invented them. Mr. Oven? Or Mrs. Oven.

ARTHUR: What did they eat before that?

MRS. PLUM: Good question, darling. Raw food I suppose.

ARTHUR: Sushi?

MR. PLUM: Sandwiches.

MRS. PLUM: Chocolate.

There is a rustling offstage.

MOLL: Hardy?

MANZ: Careful Moll, it might be an animal.

The rustling gets nearer.

HARDY enters, ragged and battered.

HARDY: I did it.

MRS. PLUM: Well done!

MR. PLUM: Very well done!

MOLL: Where is it? What did you kill?

HARDY: Here.

He takes out a dead hedgehog from his bag.

Pause.

HARDY: It fought like a cunt, but I got him in the end. Broke his neck.

Pause.

HARDY: I tracked it to its burrow. I looked for its prints in the dirt then followed them.

MR. PLUM: The prickles must have stung a lot when you grabbed it.

HARDY: They did actually.

Silence.

MRS. PLUM: Do you think there were any more where this one came from?

HARDY: It's a start isn't it?

MRS. PLUM: Oh yes. A very good start.

MR. PLUM: Very good.

HARDY: Let's cook it then. Where's the fire?

MOLL: There was some trouble getting it lit.

MANZ: There's no fuel, no paper or anything. The wood won't catch. The leaves just make smoke.

HARDY: This whole time you couldn't get a fire started?

MANZ: It's impossible. It won't catch. We'll just have to enjoy this *feast* raw.

HARDY: Is there something wrong with my hedgehog?

MANZ: It's not going to go very far.

HARDY: It's a start.

MANZ: It's a starter. It's fun-sized. It's a happy meal. You've got a *gun*, I thought you'd at least bring back a rabbit or something, a bird. The amount of time you took we were holding out for a deer.

HARDY: I hunted.

MANZ: I'll hunt. I can hunt. I'll do better than *this*.

HARDY: Yeah of course you will you weed. What were you doing when I've been out getting this? You think this was easy? I had to *hound* this. I *tracked* it down. I crawled through bushes and shrubs and up trees and into trenches and swum though rivers. I got it. I *provided* it.

MANZ: It's a fucking hedgehog! What are we going to do with a hedgehog between six of us? You're a real commando. A real fucking Rambo.

HARDY: Yeah I am, yeah I am. I am a fucking commando. I *killed* this hedgehog. I *killed* it so Moll could eat. I found its shitty little hole and I reached my arm into it and it bit me and squealed at me but I pulled it out and snapped its little neck so Moll could eat!

MANZ: If we don't find something proper to eat we're going to starve. You were supposed to keep us alive. We need a meal, not a fucking *amuse-bouche*. We need an animal!

There is a rustling sound from offstage.

Enter OCADO MAN.

The OCADO MAN stands upstage centre. He is bedraggled, his uniform is torn to shreds and he is shell-shocked. In his hands are colour-coded plastic bags.

They stare at him.

MOLL: It's Ocados!

OCADO MAN: Miss Crane?

MOLL: Yes.

OCADO MAN: Good.

They run to him and grab the bags, desperately looking for anything they can get out of them. They're empty.

I was attacked. My van was useless, stuck in a bog, stuck in Parson's Road. I left it there you see. I set out on foot. I got told, Mr. Sanderson told me, another complaint from a customer, another missed order, and I was liable to get the sack. To get fired. He said he'd hook me if it happened again. I didn't want to risk it. It's the whole company that's at stake, that's what Sanderson says. I'm a representative of the whole company, so I'm not to let them down. It's actually quite a responsibility when you think of it. I'm an ambassador. So it's up to me to provide the goods, to get them to the address. Well, that's why I set out on foot. It was alright at first. Headed down Alders Way, towards the Corn Exchange. I'd planned to nip round the back of the Odeon and come at you that way. I'd say it was almost pretty. Quite idyllic actually. There's no road anymore, but it's not like this yet. There's little saplings, bushes and reeds. The edge of Copling Street's fallen in and got filled in with rain water. There's all sorts there now, it's like a stream, trickling down the hill. Frogs, toads, beavers, fish. Dragonflies as big as my finger. And the birds! Ducks and geese and swans everywhere. Others that I don't know the names of, great big ones overhead, little ones twitching their heads at me. I stopped and had a paddle. That's where I lost my shoes. A little fox came and nicked them when I was paddling. So I pushed off from the pond barefoot. Still had all the bags at this point: fridge, cupboard,

MOLL: Freezer.

OCADO MAN: Yes, freezer. Packed full. Oh, the stuff I had for you in those bags. I mean, you'll know, you ordered it but, oh the glory! Oh lord! There was cooked hams and cured meats, diced chicken and ready-to-eat veg. I had olives for the oldies, and Fabs for the little ones. Crisps and chocolate and cereals and coffee. In the cupboard bag, I had a plastic box full of mini doughnuts. Each one was like a perfect wheel, dusted with icing sugar, delicate as snow. I tasted one. I know I shouldn't have but I got so hungry on the journey. I tasted one and – oh – it was soft, so soft, and the sugar fell into my mouth as if the very air had been sweetened. I let the dough dissolve in my mouth, I let my saliva sit with it, let it soak until I had to swallow the whole thing down.

They got me outside Habitat. It was forest by that point. So dark and dense, like this. There was barely anything left of the shop, but I could see the remains of sofas, stuck in the branches of a birch. An armchair, right up high, with a warbling robin nesting in its back. They ripped the food from the bags, even the frozen stuff. They knocked me to the ground and kicked and bit and scratched me. I tried to hold on. I thought about what Mr. Sanderson would say when I got back to the depot. I knew it was the end, he'd throw me out on my ear. But they were too strong, too many. They ate in front of my face. They gobbled it down like wolves. They crammed the fruit and veg into their hungry mouths. They tore open the bagels and the pitta bread and ate them in two bites. They moaned and growled in ecstacy. And they fed their young with the crisps and the raw meat. The milk ran down their throats and down their necks in great rivers, sticky and thick. Crème fraiche, pork pies, oven pizzas, gone. And when they had finished, when there was not so much as a puff of dusty sugar left in the air, they left me, face down in the earth, my wrist sprained, my nose bloodied. I didn't know what else to do, so I went on. And I did it. I made it here. And I saved something. I did manage to save something.

Slowly, he removes from under his shirt, a microwave chicken jalfrezi.

He holds it out to MOLL.

Slowly, MANZ, takes it from the OCADO MAN and presents it to MOLL.

Tenderly, quietly, MOLL removes the paper sleeve and the plastic top. She looks around for a fork or a knife but knows there isn't one there to find. She rolls up her sleeve and delicate as if she were stitching lace, begins to eat the ready meal with her hands. The others gather round and she feeds them too, allowing them to dip their hands in and take rice and chicken and gravy.

At length, they're done.

HARDY: It's not enough.

The OCADO MAN collapses to his knees and stares outwards.

Silence.

They all look at him.

Silence.

MR. PLUM: He'll be fired if he does ever make it back.

Pause.

MRS. PLUM: Clive's right, he'll be out on his ear, that's what he said.

MR. PLUM: He'd be finished.

Pause.

HARDY: Unless we have a fire, it doesn't matter.

MANZ: I'll get the fire going. I will, I'll get it going.

MR. PLUM: We'll all help. Arthur'll get brushwood, won't you Arthur?

He nods.

Pause.

HARDY: He'll never make it back.

MRS. PLUM: Someone'll have him if we won't.

MANZ: He's barely got a breath in him anyway.

Pause. MOLL is apart sitting by a tree. The others are either side of OCADO MAN. They all look at each other. They're in agreement.

They look to MOLL.

Pause.

MOLL: He'd be out on his ear.

Pause. They approach the OCADO MAN. Now swaying on his knees with exhaustion.

They have him surrounded, all standing above him in an open circle.

Pause.

They look at each other.

MRS. PLUM: Well…

HARDY: Right…

Pause.

MANZ, feebly raises his arm to strike. He gives the OCADO MAN a little hit on the head.

OCADO MAN: Ow.

MRS. PLUM: Come on!

MANZ: What do you mean come on?!

HARDY: Look, we need a – a rock or something.

They scatter to try to find a rock.

MR. PLUM: There's nothing here.

MRS. PLUM: It's just leaves and grass.

The OCADO MAN is wobbling to his feet. He tries to leave, but flops to his knees again.

MRS. PLUM: Come on!

HARDY: I'm thinking!

MANZ strides back up to OCADO MAN, with determination. He takes a deep breath, raises his hand to strike, swipes, but at the last minute checks himself and ends up just rapping him on the head again.

OCADO MAN: Ow. Please stop doing that.

HARDY: Shut up. Just shut up, I'm trying to think. The bags! The shopping bags!

He grabs one of the Ocado bags and wraps it around his fists, pulling it taut.

He approaches the OCADO MAN and attempts to strangle him. It works a bit, but soon, the bag rips.

HARDY: Arrrgh.

MANZ: Arrrrgh! *(He approaches the man again, really tries to gee himself up to do it, but again just ends up hitting him quite lightly on the head.)* Fucking hell!

MR. PLUM: Look. Look. He's nearly gone. He's not far now. Let's just wait. Sit it out and soon he'll do it all by himself.

They look around. No one's got any better ideas.

They all go to the bases of various trees and sit and wait.

A long silence.

MOLL: So how's it going?

MANZ: He's a survivor.

MOLL: Right. So what's the plan?

HARDY: We're waiting it out.

MOLL: Ah. How noble.

MANZ: It's more dignified.

HARDY: For him.

MANZ: Yes. Well, and for us.

Silence.

MOLL: And has there been any progress?

OCADO MAN gives a little cough.

MANZ: Some.

Silence.

MRS. PLUM: Ahem. Maybe we should play a game to pass the time?

HARDY: I really don't think that's…

MANZ: It doesn't feel quite…

Silence.

The OCADO MAN stumbles to his feet. The group watch. He stumbles slowly towards where he came from.

MRS. PLUM: He's getting away!

ARTHUR stands up. He is holding Hardy's gun. He picks up a large branch from the would-be fire and approaches the OCADO MAN from behind. He uses the branch to swipe the OCADO MAN's legs from beneath him. The OCADO MAN collapses and ARTHUR shoots him in the head three times.

Pause.

ARTHUR: There.

MRS. PLUM: Well done darling. Well done.

Silence.

iv)

The wood, later. There is blood on their hands and clothes.

HARDY is staring at his hands.

A sound offstage.

MRS. PLUM: What's that?

A sound offstage.

MRS. PLUM: What is it Clive?

MR. PLUM: I don't know Mary, do I?

A third sound.

MRS. PLUM: I can't stay here.

MR. PLUM: Where would you like to go?

MRS. PLUM: Where's Tim? Let's try to find Tim.

MR. PLUM: Mary.

MRS. PLUM: Arthur. Come here. It's time to go on another adventure now alright. Mummy and Daddy want to go on another adventure.

ARTHUR: Where to?

MRS. PLUM: To find Uncle Tim. Won't that be nice?

MR. PLUM: That's right. We might go to find Uncle Tim. He's a bit of a journey away though, that's all. So we might have to go on a bit of a journey to find him.

ARTHUR: Is Moll coming with us?

MRS. PLUM: Moll has to stay here. This is where she lives.

ARTHUR: This is where we live too, now.

MANZ: It's a bear.

MRS. PLUM: A bear!

MANZ: The smell of the meat. It's attracting animals.

HARDY: No.

MANZ: It won't come into the camp yet, the noise will make it suspicious.

HARDY: It's just a matter of time.

MR. PLUM: Since when did we have bears in England?

MANZ: About a week ago I read there was a sighting at Plymouth. I didn't think they'd get this far north this quickly.

MRS. PLUM: There it is again!

ARTHUR: I'll kill it.

MRS. PLUM: No darling.

ARTHUR: Yes I will I'll have it. Lend me the gun again, I'll do it in.

MANZ: This one's a job for grown-ups. Stay here. Hardy and I'll go.

HARDY: OK.

MANZ: Come on Hardy. Let's go.

MR. PLUM: Why does anyone have to go? There'll be more after that one anyway. Can't we try and escape? Head north and try to outrun the seeds.

HARDY: There's no chance of that. It's spread too quickly.

MANZ: Besides…

MR. PLUM: Yes?

MRS. PLUM: What is it?

Pause.

HARDY: Tell them.

MANZ: This morning. After. When you were all still sleeping. Hardy and I tried to forage for something to eat. We couldn't pull up any of the plants, all the leaves were too tough but we were desperate. So we kept looking. We must have gone almost a mile north when we saw it. They've built a wall. A plastic wall as high as the canopy. Redwoods, oaks and pines are pressed to it, their roots are crunching against it. The army must have encircled us. Given up the South and tried to stop the seed spreading any further.

MR. PLUM: Well that's good news. There must be a door, a checkpoint somewhere?

HARDY: There is.

MR. PLUM: So? Let's go.

Pause.

MR. PLUM: Well?

HARDY: They won't have the boy. And they won't have Moll.

MANZ: To get through the checkpoint you have to be decontaminated. But it's heavy stuff. They won't do it to any one they think is…frail.

MRS. PLUM: Of course they will.

HARDY: There were dozens of children there. Abandoned the wrong side of the wall. They won't let them through.

MRS. PLUM: No.

MR. PLUM: That sound again. It's getting closer.

Pause.

MANZ: Let's go. Hardy?

HARDY: We have to.

MANZ: Clive?

MR. PLUM: Yes. Alright.

MRS. PLUM: Oh Clive.

They make to leave.

MOLL: Won't you need the gun?

They stop. They go to take it from her.

MOLL: Good luck.

They go.

A long silence. MOLL and ARTHUR sit together.

MRS. PLUM watches them.

MOLL: When Hardy was a little boy he used to sit by the window and kill flies. Smudge them into the glass. Manz would sit and watch him. Hours and hours. They must have got through a hundred flies a day at their peak. They'll be alright.

Another long silence.

ARTHUR: Do you know what this is?

He takes the green Ocado bag and floats it through the air.

MOLL: No. What is it?

ARTHUR: A dragon.

MOLL smiles.

MOLL: Once upon a time there were two dragons sitting together in the forest. Suddenly a knight in shining armour came walking into the glade. The first dragon looked at his mate and said, 'Breakfast!'. The second replied 'Nah, I don't feel like canned food'.

They smile. MRS. PLUM smiles.

MR. PLUM re-enters.

MR PLUM: They did it.

ARTHUR: They killed the bear?

MR. PLUM: Yes darling, they killed the bear.

ARTHUR: How?

MR. PLUM: They approached it from behind. It was asleep.

ARTHUR: Why was it making so much noise then? Are you sure it was the right bear?

MR. PLUM: It was tired from making all the noise. It was the right bear. It woke up anyway, made a noise. The same noise.

ARTHUR: Was it big?

MR. PLUM: As big as Mum's Astra. It stood up on its back legs. It roared. Hardy shot it.

ARTHUR: Where?

MR. PLUM: Here. Through the neck. It fell on the ground and the tree shook.

ARTHUR: Where was it?

MR. PLUM: Just near here. It was coming for the man. We got it just in time.

ARTHUR: Why didn't we hear the gun?

MR. PLUM: It had a silencer on. It was ever so quiet. Hardy didn't want to disturb the other animals and attract attention. He was very brave. Very brave.

ARTHUR: Are they bringing the bear back? Will we eat it?

MR. PLUM: No. It's too heavy.

ARTHUR: So shall we go and eat it there?

MR. PLUM: We can't eat it. It was poisoned. From the berries it was eating.

ARTHUR: Where are the boys?

MR. PLUM: With the bear. Making sure it's dead.

ARTHUR: Why didn't they come back with you?

MR. PLUM: They wanted to make sure the bear was dead. So you were safe. Look, they'll be back soon with bear steaks. They're going to cut off some big juicy bear steaks and bring them back here for breakfast.

MRS. PLUM: Won't that be nice?

ARTHUR: But won't they be poisoned?

MR. PLUM: They'll be careful to cut only from the clean side. So if you have a rest, get some sleep, and then before you know it, it will be time for the best breakfast you've ever had.

ARTHUR: OK. I want to sleep over here with Moll. Moll, why are you crying?

MRS. PLUM: She's very proud of her boys.

ARTHUR: Me too.

ARTHUR goes over to lie by MOLL.

MR. PLUM looks at MRS. PLUM.

He makes an incomprehensible signal with his eyes.

She doesn't understand.

He tries again, it's even more incomprehensible.

She still doesn't understand.

He tries again.

She understands.

They look at ARTHUR, lying on MOLL.

Silence.

MRS. PLUM goes to ARTHUR.

MRS. PLUM: Sweet dreams, Arthur. Sweet dreams.

Blackout.

v)

The wood, the next morning. Only MOLL and ARTHUR are there.

MOLL is awake, ARTHUR is asleep in her lap.

Silence.

MOLL: Got it. Ahem.

What's the difference between a hen night and a trip to the zoo?

Well one's full of loud, hairy animals being poked in public by men in uniform.

And the other has a gift shop.

ARTHUR wakes up.

He looks around. They are alone. MR. and MRS. PLUM are nowhere to be seen.

ARTHUR looks behind a tree. He returns to the camp.

Pause.

He goes to another tree and looks around there too, before returning to camp.

Silence.

ARTHUR: Tell me about King Arthur again.

MOLL: I don't know very much.

ARTHUR: Was he strong?

MOLL: I expect so.

ARTHUR: And brave?

MOLL: Yes. He was very brave.

ARTHUR: Did he kill and stab people he didn't like.

MOLL: No. He was very generous. Even his best friend, who betrayed him and stole his wife.

ARTHUR: Gingerbeer?

MOLL: Yes, Gingerbeer. He didn't even kill him.

ARTHUR: When was that? The Second World War?

MOLL: No, before that. When England still had lions and dragons and fairy tale princesses. When ghosts rustled in the trees. There weren't streets. There weren't shops. Just copses and brooks and clearings and dells.

ARTHUR: And castles?

MOLL: Big castles by the sea or on hills.

From offstage there is the sound of frenzied whooping and shouting. It is the sound of children. Tens, maybe hundreds of children, careering through the forest, wild and war-like.

ARTHUR rushes to the edge of the clearing to see. He places himself between the sound and MOLL.

ARTHUR: Children.

MOLL: Must be hundreds of them.

ARTHUR: Laughing.

MOLL: Going to attack the wall?

ARTHUR: Wicked.

ARTHUR takes a step towards the forest. Then stops.

MOLL: Why aren't you running?

ARTHUR: I can't.

MOLL: Why?

ARTHUR: I have to stay here.

MOLL: Why?

ARTHUR: In case anything happens. I have to stay here in case.

Another whooping group of children pass.

MOLL and ARTHUR listen to the sounds disappear into the distance.

Silence.

MOLL: Thank you.

ARTHUR: Do you think Nicole Clark is on this side of the wall? I hope she got through.

MOLL is looking in her handbag. She takes out her blusher.

Why are you still putting on your make-up?

MOLL: To look beautiful.

ARTHUR: I think you are beautiful. For a grandma.

MOLL: Thank you.

ARTHUR kisses her on the lips.

MOLL: You should have gone with the kids.

ARTHUR: Your face feels loose. Loose and dry.

MOLL takes from her bag one of the lispalves that were looted earlier and applies it.

They kiss again.

ARTHUR: That's a bit better.

MOLL: Thank you.

ARTHUR: You're not as good a kisser as Shadima from class six.

MOLL gets out her cigarettes.

MOLL: Last one.

ARTHUR: Shall we twos it?

MOLL: Yes.

She puts it in her mouth and then realises she has nothing to light it with.

The boy gets up, roots around the dead fire and finds the box of matches.

ARTHUR: There's one left.

MOLL: Yes.

Carefully, he strikes the match and, with it, the cigarette. They watch the match burn to the end, and he throws it away.

They smoke.

There is a sound from offstage. A rustling of leaves.

The BRIDE enters. She is dressed in a pink T-shirt which enhances her cleavage, and a miniskirt. On the back of the T-Shirt reads 'The Bride'. She is wearing a cheap plastic crown. She is clutching a piece of paper in her hand.

ARTHUR: Moll, look. There *are* still princesses in the forest. She's got the most beautiful tits I've ever seen. She looks like a porn star!

MOLL: She's not a real princess.

ARTHUR: Yes she is. A real princess. She's like all my dreams have come true. I bet she's easy. I bet she's gagging for it, Moll. Is *this* what love is?

MOLL: Yes.

ARTHUR: Are you jealous Moll? Are you jealous because she's so young and I don't fancy you?

MOLL: Yes.

ARTHUR: But you're not interested in sex are you Moll? Not any more. Not like her. Look at her skirt.

MOLL: It's a very nice skirt.

ARTHUR: You are a real princess aren't you?

The BRIDE opens her mouth to speak, but nothing comes out. She tries again, but nothing comes again.

The piece of paper drops from her hand. ARTHUR picks it up and hands it to MOLL.

MOLL: *(Reading.)* 'I'm getting married tomorrow! Before I get hitched I must complete six tasks: One. Snog a bald man.

The BRIDE nods.

Two. Get a man's pants.

The BRIDE holds up some men's pants. They have blood on them.

Three. Swap an item of clothing with a man.

She holds up a bloody shirt.

Get a man to flash his bum at me.

She nods, and cries.

Enjoy one last kiss of freedom: snog the sexiest guy in the club.

She looks at the ARTHUR, collecting herself. She goes to him and kisses him slowly on the lips.

Last one. Enjoy one last dance of freedom: slow dance with the sexiest guy in the club.'

She takes out her phone and begins to play some music.

She looks at ARTHUR. He holds her by the waist and they dance, slowly and romantically.

Music surges.

ARTHUR lets go of the bride and turns to face MOLL. He approaches her and holds her waist. They begin to dance.

The bride picks up the discarded list of tasks. She looks at them, then looks out.

BRIDE: Mum, Dad, Alex, Kate, and everyone who's come tonight. I want to first thank Mum so much for organising this evening. And Dad for paying for it. But most of all I want to thank you, Scott. Thank you for being the love of my life. Thank you for making your vows to me and for allowing me to make mine to you. We will wake up tomorrow next to each other and our lives will never be the same. I want to be with you for the rest of my life. And I can't wait. The world seems fresh, full and alive. Birds are singing, the sun is shining. And we have a whole new future ahead of us.

Music continues.

    Curtain.

APPENDIX

[note: getting a chorus of children is expensive and difficult. However, if you can, the section in part 3 where ARTHUR hears the children can also be played as follows.]

From offstage there is frenzied whooping and shouting. It is the sound of children. Tens, maybe hundreds of children, careering through the forest, wild and war-like.

ARTHUR rushes to the edge of the clearing to see. He places himself between the sound and Moll.

Suddenly a six-year-old boy runs straight across stage from left to right, whooping like a Red Indian.

As soon as he disappears, more enter: a stampede of children cascade across stage. They look wild and war-like. They are out of control. MOLL is almost bowled over, ARTHUR tries to place himself between them and her.

In the frenzy, the children barely notice MOLL and ARTHUR. At length (15, 30, 80? – note: a trick of revolving the same children around the back of the stage could allow for a stampede as long as a piece of string – especially if they were camouflaged with leaves and branches) a very young boy notices ARTHUR. He stops. Five or six other young children stop too.

There is now a group of children facing ARTHUR who is standing in front of MOLL.

BOY 1: Why aren't you running?

Silence.

GIRL 1: We're going to attack the wall.

BOY 1: Ben Maloney's the leader. He found a gun.

Pause.

GIRL 2: You should come. It's going to be wicked.

Pause. ARTHUR takes a step towards them. Then stops.

ARTHUR: I can't.

GIRL 1: Why?

ARTHUR: I have to stay here.

GIRL 1: Why?

ARTHUR: In case anything happens. I have to stay here in case.

Another whooping group of children pass through.

GIRL 1: Well, bye.

BOY 1: Bye!

They run off with the others, cheering and shouting.

MOLL and ARTHUR listen to the sounds disappear into the distance.

Silence.

MOLL: Thank you.

Acknowledgements

For my grandparents, who were clearly on my mind.
With thanks to Jay and Lu for reading it early; Nina, Sarah
and everyone at Soho for working so hard on its behalf;
Steve and all the cast and crew for bringing so much to the
table. Mum, Dad, Charlie and Rose for constant support;
and Valentina for making the ending go pah…

WWW.OBERONBOOKS.COM

Follow us on www.twitter.com/@oberonbooks
& www.facebook.com/oberonbook